COME INTO THE KITCHEN

E. M. S.

from

J. N. G. S.

27/3/48.

COME
INTO THE KITCHEN

A
Cookery Book
for Boys & Girls

By

ALEXIE GORDON & TRUDY BLISS

Drawings by
NANCY INNES

LONDON
VICTOR GOLLANCZ LTD
1947

TO

HENRIETTA AND PHILIP,

BARBARA AND KAREN

Printed in Great Britain by
The Camelot Press Ltd., London and Southampton

Contents

CHAP.   PAGE

Introductory Note 7

I. Come into the Kitchen 9

II. Afternoon Tea with Buttered Toast . . 13

III. Afternoon Tea with Scones 17

IV. Get Your Own Supper 21

V. Saturday Lunch 24

VI. Elevenses 27

VII. Sweet Herbs 32

VIII. The Salad Bowl 35

IX. A Friend to Tea 40

X. French Vegetable Soup 45

XI. Stew in Oven, Semolina Pudding. . . 49

XII. Sunday Supper 52

XIII. Pastry 57

XIV. Cauliflower Cheese 61

XV. Another Dish with White Sauce . . . 64

XVI. The Lighter Side of Cooking—Fudge . . 66

XVII. Blackberry Jam 69

XVIII. A Picnic 72

XIX. Eggs and Bacon 76

XX. Five Festivals 78

XXI. Cook-books and Recipes 85

Index of Recipes 100

Acknowledgments

MY thanks are due to Messrs. Sidgwick and Jackson for permission to quote from the poems of Rupert Brooke and John Drinkwater; to Miss Eleanor Farjeon for permission to print her poem "Sweet Herbs" (published by Faber and Faber); to Mrs. C. F. Leyel and Miss Olga Hartley for permission to quote from *The Gentle Art of Cookery* (published by Messrs. Chatto and Windus); to Major Francis Brett Young for permission to quote from his book, *The Island* (published by Heinemann).

I would like to thank Mrs. Arthur Webb for allowing me to use her recipe for mincemeat on p. 83.

Lastly, I would like to acknowledge my debt of gratitude to Lydia Horton for her kindness in checking over the recipes.

T. B.

Introductory Note

THE original idea of this book was Alexie Gordon's. The plan of it was hers, and it was she who wrote the greater part of it. I was to contribute the recipes. When she died a year ago, the book was nearly complete, and, working from her notes, I have tried to finish it according to her design.

We both agreed that we would make this recommendation to mothers: "When your child is cooking, don't *hover*. Don't make suggestions, unless, of course, your advice is asked. Just relax and wait for the proud achievement."

TRUDY BLISS.

December, 1946.

CHAPTER I

Come into the Kitchen

YOU know that delicious smell of newly baked bread which fills the kitchen after the lovely creamy loaves have been removed from the oven? It finds its way through open doors, flavouring the whole house, and at home on baking days I always wandered into the kitchen to see what was going on. This has happened for generations—my mother was irresistibly drawn into the kitchen on baking day to see what my grandmother was doing, and my grandmother, if she was not already in the big old-fashioned kitchen with her frilly little cap and apron on, perhaps ran downstairs to sniff delightedly at a batch of scones lying like little pools of light on a corner of the black polished kitchen range. What a delightful place the kitchen is, and how full of surprises! But how it has changed with the centuries! There have been many famous and beautiful kitchens, and perhaps one day you will see some of them. Perhaps you will visit the great Tudor kitchens at Hampton Court and Christ Church, Oxford, the former no longer in use, but the

Oxford kitchen still bustling with the preparation of meals for the college; or the lovely kitchen in the Royal Palace at Cintra in Portugal with its two beautiful conical chimneys rising beyond the ceiling. However, I can't believe that any kitchen is as alluring as your own, with its shiny pots and pans, its pretty earthenware casseroles and gay china. In spring it is perhaps you who have picked the primroses to fill that brown bowl on the window-sill, and in summer you may have pricked your fingers gathering the roses for the vases; and do you like the nutty scent of the geraniums when you water them in winter? How warm and cosy the kitchen is in winter! An occasional coal drops through the iron bars of the grate and a little purple flame flickers for a second in a friendly way. Then there is the comforting thought of those cupboard doors and the rosy jars of jams and jellies, golden bottles of fruit and rich-looking preserves which stand in neat rows on the shelves behind them.

Well, here we are in the kitchen, where there are certainly plenty of things to look at. You hardly need an introduction to the teapot and kettle, or the coffee-pot and jugs. How comfortable they all look sitting there waiting to be used! And the saucepans and frying pans—you'll be using them a lot if you start cooking in a serious way. The mixing bowl is very important, for its sloping sides slant in just such a way as to make mixing a cake or a pudding with one of those wooden spoons as easy as possible. That brings us to the cake tins and patty pans. Look at them and think how nice they will be with a golden cake or some pretty  brown scones well risen inside them! The knives, spoons, forks and perforated soup ladle, the apple-corer, and the tin-opener are all in this drawer—and the fish slice too; and there in the cupboard are the plates, dishes and casseroles, with the cups dangling from the shelf above. Then here is the colander and the wire sieves, the mincer and the grater—the last is essential to the modern cook, as it is used for grating raw vegetables and fruits for salads in summer as well as food that is going to be cooked. Don't you like the sound of the egg-beater whirring away in a basin of frothy yellow egg? We must be grateful to it for the time and labour it saves. And here is the rolling pin, almost as useful to the comedian as to the cook, but I hope *you* won't be hitting anyone on the head with it!

A word about the scales. What fun it is to measure out exactly the amounts of the ingredients you need for your recipes! If your scales are the kind that have separate weights, take care of them—don't let them roll on the kitchen floor and get lost or you will be in for trouble when your mother comes to do her cooking!

And now the alarm clock—don't look surprised; you will find it most useful to time your baking. It is so easy to forget the exact time your cake should emerge from the oven, so have the alarm clock set for the correct time and when it goes off with a whirr you will be reminded that there, in the oven, is a cake waiting to be looked at.

There are still other utensils in the kitchen that I have not mentioned, but they are not ones that you will use very often, so I will introduce them later when you will be needing them.

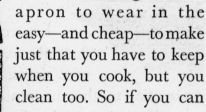

Have you got a pretty apron to wear in the kitchen? If not, it is very easy—and cheap—to make one. Remember, it is not just that you have to keep yourself neat and clean when you cook, but you have to keep your food clean too. So if you can

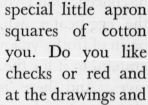

manage it, keep a special little apron for cooking. Two squares of cotton gingham will do you. Do you like blue and white checks or red and white checks? Look at the drawings and you will see how easy it is. Gather the middle of the big square and fit the little square on to it and there you are. Then a strip of tape or of the material to go round your neck and two strips to tie round your waist.

At the head of each recipe I have made a list of the ingredients and utensils you will need. Get them all out before you start to cook. By doing this you will be sure that you have all the ingredients required and you will save yourself fuss and flurry in following the directions.

The general recipes in this book will make enough to serve four people.

CHAPTER II

Afternoon Tea with Buttered Toast

"I did send for a cup of tea, a Chinese drink, of which I never had drunk before."

PEPYS: *Diary*, September 25th, 1660

TEA was first brought to England at the end of the sixteenth century, and by the middle of the next century the richer classes were buying it and drinking it. The price was anything from £6 to £10 a pound, which explains why ladies kept it carefully in tea caddies in the drawing-room and not in the kitchen store cupboard.

If you have read *Cranford,* you will remember how Miss Matty became an agent for the East India Tea Company and set up her little shop to sell tea to the neighbouring gentry.

Little rows of canisters with such romantic names as Pekoe, Congou and Souchong lined her shelves. There was an extra fine and expensive brand called Gunpowder, which has always seemed to me an oddly named tea for the genteel tables of those times.

Does your mother like India or China tea in the afternoon? Find the canister of tea she prefers, and this is how you make it, serving it for a treat on that little tray with some hot buttered toast and jam.

13

TEA

(Allow 15 minutes)

Ingredients	*Utensils*
Tea.	Teapot.
Boiling water.	Teacup.
	Teaspoon.
	Tea kettle.

1. Fill the tea kettle and set it on the stove to heat.
2. While you are waiting for the kettle to boil, it's a good idea to see how many cups of water your teapot holds. Use the teacup to fill it up. Then you can judge how much to put in when you actually make the tea. Suppose you are making tea for two people and you think they will each have two cups of tea, put in four cupfuls of water and remember how far up on the inside the level comes.
3. Now with hot water from the tap, if you have it, fill up your pot and let it stand till the pot is really warm. Use water from the kettle if it doesn't run hot from the tap.
4. Now, is your kettle boiling, really boiling, not just humming?
5. If it is, pour away the water from the pot and—
6. Measure into the pot 1 level teaspoon of tea for each cup you plan to put in. 4 cups of water, 4 teaspoonfuls of tea (level teaspoonfuls, not heaped up).

14

7. Put the lid tightly on the canister of tea, so that the goodness won't escape.
8. Pour the boiling water on to the tea in the pot.
9. Don't forget to turn out the stove.
10. Put the teapot on the tray and serve with—

HOT BUTTERED TOAST
(Allow 15 minutes)

Ingredients	*Utensils*
A loaf of bread (stale if you have it).	Bread board.
	Bread knife.
Butter.	Butter knife.
	Plate.

1. Cut slices of bread about $\frac{1}{4}$ inch thick.
2. Cut the slices in half. (It's better to do this before you toast it; it cuts easier.)
3. Light the toasting grill of your stove.
4. Lay the pieces of bread on the little rack and put them under the flame (about 1 inch away is best).
5. Watch like a hawk!
6. When they are brown on one side, turn them over and toast on the other.
7. Spread with butter and—
8. Pile on the plate in neat piles.
9. Turn out the stove.
10. Put away the bread knife

and the bread board and the bread back into the bin.
Brush up any crumbs you may have made.

11. Serve.

It is quite an art to lay a tray and make it look really attractive
and it is no matter if all the china doesn't match, but choose
pieces that look well together. The teapot, of course, a little milk
jug and sugar basin, and a tiny bowl to use as a slop basin; a
plate and knife, cup and saucer and spoon, and then the little
jam dish filled with some favourite jam, and a spoon to serve it
with. And don't forget the hot-water jug. Now, is everything
ready? Is there room for a tiny vase of flowers, or could you lay
just one rose on the tray to make it look gay?

CHAPTER III

Afternoon Tea with Scones

"Stands the Church clock at ten to three?
And is there honey still for tea?"

RUPERT BROOKE, the young English poet who was killed in the Great War of 1914-18, finished up a poem with these lines. He was sitting in a *café* in Berlin one very hot day, and, though I dare say he really was enjoying himself, he couldn't help thinking how nice and cool it must be in the tiny English village of Grantchester on the River Cam. He thought of the lovely flowers and the cool water and the hospitable Vicarage where he used to visit. Not many other countries besides England make such a feature of the meal we have in the afternoon—tea. I am sure at the Vicarage they had freshly baked scones to spread with that sweet honey. Scones are  really quite easy to make, and they are always appreciated by those who sit down to eat them. The most difficult part is the rubbing of the fat into the flour, but I feel sure you will be able to manage it. If you can bake them in the afternoon, so much the better, then they might even be warm when you put them on the table. In the summer, when it is hot, there is often a little sour milk in the larder. If there is and it can be spared, you should use it to make the dough. Then the scones will be extra light and delicious.

Here is the recipe—follow it carefully.

SCONES

(Allow half an hour)

Ingredients	Utensils
½ lb. self-raising flour.	Mixing bowl.
¼ teaspoon salt.	Baking sheet.
1½ level tablespoons	Bit of greaseproof paper.
margarine.	Medium size sieve.
¼ pint milk.	Fork.
	Rolling pin.
	Round scone-cutter (the rim of a small glass will do if you haven't a scone-cutter).
	Tablespoon.
	Teaspoon.
	Pint jug.
	Scales.

1. Light the oven and set it to "hot."
2. Take a little margarine or lard on the piece of greaseproof paper and grease your baking sheet well with it, so that the scones won't stick as they cook.
3. Now sift the flour and the salt together into your mixing bowl.
4. Measure out the margarine and add it to your flour.

5. Now, using the tips of your fingers (you did wash your hands before you began to cook, didn't you?), rub the margarine into the flour, just lightly.
6. When the flour and margarine are nicely mixed so that the little lumps are the size of breadcrumbs, add the milk, mixing it in with the fork till the dough is soft.
7. Dust the board and rolling pin lightly with flour and lift your dough out on to it.
8. Roll out flat with the rolling pin. Don't press down too hard or the rolling pin will stick to the dough.
9. Roll out till the dough is $\frac{3}{4}$ inch thick.
10. Dip the scone-cutter or the edge of your small glass into a little heap of flour and cut out your rounds.
11. Lay them on the greased baking sheet.
12. Now pick up the odd pieces of dough left and pat them together into one piece and roll out again. Cut out more rounds, and so on until the dough is used up.
13. Put the baking sheet in the hot oven and cook for 10 minutes.
14. While the scones are cooking, tidy up the kitchen table. Did you spill any flour on the floor? It's awfully hard not to, so wipe it up and leave the kitchen spick and span.
15. Take out your scones and turn out the oven.

Have you got a small sister or brother who likes playing with dolls and perhaps has quite a large family of them? If so, you should give them a dolls' tea party one day. Make the same mixture, but only half the quantity. Now roll the dough thinner. Instead of cutting the scones out with the ordinary scone-cutter, use a thimble instead (the largest one you can find), and then, when you have placed these tiny scones on your baking sheet and put them in the oven, let them bake for 5 minutes only. If you have alpine strawberries in your garden, gather a little dish of these to serve with the scones. Wild strawberries will do as well, of course. If it is not the season for strawberries, what about sultanas or raisins? I am sure the party will be a great success.

CHAPTER IV

Get Your Own Supper

"At the top of the house the apples are laid in rows
And the skylight lets the moonlight in, and those
Apples are deep-sea apples of green."
                                        JOHN DRINKWATER.

WHAT a useful and kindly fruit the apple is! When it is first being harvested in the early autumn, it can be eaten crisp and fresh from the tree. And then, all through the winter, over the festive Christmas season and well into spring, certain kinds can be stored and used when wanted. Here is a basketful of large, round, mellow-looking apples. Do you remember the orchard last spring? Here and there a few petals floated to the ground as you stood under the branches looking at the blue sky through the delicate blossoms, and I wonder if you gave a thought to the winter and the loft where the apples lay in rows . . . under the gloomy beams; on the sagging floor?

Like most fruits, the apple is easy to cook, but, unlike many other English fruits, it can be baked. Then it still looks like an apple, though its middle has been removed and its skin, more yellow and pink than before, is all wrinkled and puckered. Why not have it as your pudding for supper on an evening when your mother is going out? This, of course, is starting the meal backwards, which is not at all correct. Hastily, we must think of a first course. Did you collect the eggs to-day? If so, you will know whether any can be spared for your supper to-night. New laid eggs boiled are so good, and toast fingers go well with them. Then there's a beaker of milk for each of you.

28/9/57.

BAKED APPLES
(Allow 45 minutes)

Ingredients	Utensils
4 apples.	Apple-corer or a sharp-pointed
2 level tablespoons sugar	knife.
(brown or white).	Shallow casserole or baking tin.
A little hot water.	Long-handled spoon.
	Tablespoon.

1. Light the oven and set it to "hot."
2. If the apples are bought from a shop, wash them first, but if they are off your own trees you don't have to bother, do you?

3. Push the apple-corer through from the stem end to the end where the little bit of blossom still shows. Try to get out all the core, as it's horrid to come across those horny bits when you eat your delicious baked apple at supper.
4. Set the cored apples in the casserole or baking dish.
5. Fill the centres with the sugar.
6. Cover the bottom of the dish with hot water, about half an inch.
7. Bake it in your hot oven, and two or three times during the cooking pull the dish towards you and take up some of the syrup in a spoon. Pour it over the apples and then let them go on cooking. This pouring the juice over them with a spoon is called "basting" and keeps the skins from drying up and becoming tough.

22

8. The apples are done when they are soft through. Test with a fork. It generally takes 20 minutes to half an hour.

While the apples are baking you can cook the eggs and make the toast. The toast you already know how to make, but just remember always to watch it most carefully—it burns so easily, and then nobody wants to eat it! Now for the eggs. (And by the way, when you are serving up the supper remember to put a little plate of butter on the table, and the salt cellar.)

BOILED EGGS
(Allow 10 minutes)

Ingredients	*Utensils*
1 egg for each person.	1 large spoon.
	Clock.
	Medium-sized saucepan.
	Egg-cups.

1. Put enough water in the saucepan to cover the eggs when you come to put them in.
2. Set it on the stove to heat.
3. When the water is boiling, take each egg up in the large spoon and slip it gently into the saucepan.
4. Reduce the heat so that the water is just simmering, not boiling, and cook for 3 minutes for a soft-boiled egg and $4\frac{1}{2}$ minutes for a firm egg. If the eggs have come out of the refrigerator or a very cold larder, allow 1 minute extra.
5. Take out from the water with the spoon and set into the egg-cups.
6. Turn out the stove.

CHAPTER V

Saturday Lunch

THE potato has been called the King of the Kitchen Garden, and so it is with its decorative flowers, sometimes white and sometimes violet. It came to Europe first four hundred years ago; the Spaniards brought it from Peru. A little later Francis Drake brought potatoes to England from North America along with tobacco.

The potato might also be called the King of the Kitchen, it is so important as food. There are many ways of preparing and cooking it, but let us start with what the French call potatoes *en robe de chambre* (in their dressing gowns)—or what we call a little less fancifully, "baked potatoes." It is a very simple recipe and one that keeps all the goodness in the vegetable. Perhaps one morning your mother will allow you to share her kitchen if, in return, you do your part towards preparing the lunch. Anyway, ask her and see what she says. You might suggest that you look after the potatoes and the sweet. For a sweet you might bake apples, if the oven is already hot. You know how to do this, but could change the garnishings of your dish to make a variation. Try baking them this time with raisins—hard, wrinkled, sweet raisins when you take them from the packet, but coming out of the oven soft and gently puffed out.

24

BAKED POTATOES

(Allow 55 minutes)

Ingredients

Medium potatoes (all about the same size).

Utensils

Scrubbing brush.
The sink.
Fork.
The oven.

1. See that there is a rack about three-quarters of the way up in your oven and then turn on the heat, setting it to "hot."

2. Choose as many potatoes as you need (one for each person or two if your appetites are big). Try to pick out ones of equal size, but if some have to be bigger, cut them in half, so they'll take the same time to cook through.

3. Scrub them in warm water with the vegetable brush until no earth is left on them. Hold them well down in the sink

while you are scrubbing, otherwise the dirty water will splatter all over the front of your apron.

4. Prick each potato once with the fork. They'll be soggy if you don't.

5. Put them in the oven, which should be hot by now. Lay them on the rack spaced out, not touching each other.

6. Cook for 40 minutes. (This time depends on the size of your potatoes and the heat of your oven.) You can tell if they are done by sticking a fork into them. (Don't burn your hand in that hot oven!) If the fork goes in easily all the way and the insides feel soft, the potatoes are cooked.

CHAPTER VI

Elevenses

"Close by those Meads, forever crown'd with Flowers,
Where Thames with Pride surveys his rising Towers,
There stands a Structure of Majestic Frame,
Which from the neighbouring Hampton takes its Name[1]
Here Britain's Statesmen oft' the Fall foredoom
Of Foreign Tyrants, and of Nymphs at home;
Here Thou, Great Anna![2] whom three realms obey,
Dost sometimes Counsel take—and sometimes Tea.

*   *   *   *

For lo! the Board with Cups and Spoons is crown'd,
The Berries crackle,[3] and the Mill[4] turns round;
On shining Altars of Japan[5] they raise
The silver Lamp; and fiery Spirits blaze:
From silver Spouts the grateful Liquors glide,
While China's Earth[6] receive the smoking Tide.
At once they gratify their Scent and Taste,
And frequent Cups prolong the rich Repaste."

ALEXANDER POPE (1688–1744): *The Rape of the Lock*

WHEN you are out for the day with a friend, what fun it is to go into a little tea-shop, sit down to a cup of coffee or hot chocolate and, watch the waitress bearing down on your table with a plate piled high with cakes and chocolate biscuits! Elevenses are good at home too, and on a Sunday morning, when your father is perhaps working in the garden, he may find a steaming hot cup of some beverage made by you most welcome. Both coffee and cocoa are easy to make, but remember to take just as much care over their preparation as you would over some more complicated dish. Or on a hot summer's

[1] Hampton Court.
[2] Queen Anne.
[3] Roasting coffee berries.

[4] Coffee-grinder.
[5] Japanese lacquered tray.
[6] The clay from which Chinese porcelain is made.

day, how refreshing he would find a glass of lemonade. There are several variations, such as mint or pineapple lemonade, but the recipe you will find here uses only lemons and makes a very good iced drink.

If it is cocoa you are taking into the garden, ask your father if he knows how many flowers a full-grown cocoa tree bears, and of these flowers how many will become pods. It is quite likely he won't know, so you can have the fun of telling him that the cocoa tree bears about 6,000 small pink flowers, but of these flowers only twenty will become pods. Or, if it is a cup of stimulating coffee you are handing to him, tell him that the Turks who brought it to Europe drank it because they were not allowed by their religion to drink wine. There are many ways of making coffee, and many different machines to make it with, but this recipe you will find an easy method, involving nothing more special than an earthenware, china or enamel jug.

COFFEE
(Allow 15 minutes)

Ingredients	*Utensils*
4 oz. coffee, ground coarsely.	A 2-pint measure.
Water.	Tablespoon.
	Fine mesh strainer or a piece of butter muslin (a little piece 8 inches square will do).
	Jug with a lid to serve the coffee in.
	Saucepan.

1. Put 2 pints of water on to boil.

2. Put the coffee into the pint measure. It should come to the 4-oz. mark.

3. Fill up the measure with *boiling* water.

4. Give a vigorous stir and leave for 5 minutes.

5. Pour through the strainer or the piece of muslin into the coffee jug.

6. Put on the stove and heat it up again (really hot), but don't let it boil.

7. Serve with hot or cold milk (or cream) and sugar.

29

COCOA
(Allow 15 minutes)

Ingredients

2 level tablespoons cocoa.
2 level tablespoons granu-
lated sugar.
½ teacup cold water.
1½ pints milk.
Marshmallows (not abso-
lutely necessary, but
nice).

Utensils

Saucepan.
Small mixing basin.
Tablespoon and a wooden spoon.
Jug.
Cups.

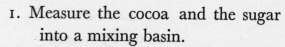

1. Measure the cocoa and the sugar into a mixing basin.

2. Add the water gradually, stirring it well in, so that the mixture is very smooth.

3. Put the milk into the saucepan and bring very gradually to the boil, stirring with the wooden spoon to keep it from burning on the bottom.

4. When it is boiling, turn the heat down and stir in the cocoa mixture.

5. Bring it to the boil again gradually, stirring all the time.

6. Serve. It is fun to put a marshmallow in each cup and pour the cocoa over it. The marshmallow will float to the top and make the cocoa extra special.

LEMONADE
(Allow 10 minutes)

Ingredients	Utensils
3 lemons.	Lemon squeezer, if you have one.
8-10 level tablespoons sugar.	Sharp knife.
	Pint measure.
1½ pints cold water.	Tablespoon.
	Small strainer.
	Jug.
	Glasses.

1. Roll the lemons on the table back and forth under the palm of your hand. This helps you squeeze the juice easily.
2. Cut the lemons in half (around the middle) and squeeze the juice into the pint jug. (Don't throw away the rinds. Your mother can use them for flavouring.)
3. Strain into the jug.
4. Add the sugar and the water.
5. Stir very well and, when the sugar is dissolved, taste the lemonade and see if it is sweet enough. If not, add more sugar.
6. If you have a refrigerator and can put in a lump of ice for each person, that would be fine.

7. A sprig of mint is nice sticking out of the top of the jug, and adds a delicate flavour.

CHAPTER VII

Sweet Herbs

What shall I plant in my little herb border?
Which of these hundred sweet names shall I order?
Mallow or Marjoram, Tansy or Rue,
Lovage or Hyssop, or Call-Me-To-You?

Thyme or Sweet Cicely, which shall I take?
Shall I plant Basil for Isabel's sake?
Betony, Bergamot, Orris, Vervain,
Chicory, Woodruff, or Elecampane?

Here's Lady's Mantle, and here is Old Man:
If I cannot plant all, I must plant what I can,
But their names throw me into delicious disorder!
What shall I plant in my little herb border?

ELEANOR FARJEON

I THINK we all love herbs. The word itself at once conjures up a picture of the past when herbs were used so much more than they are now, a picture, perhaps, of a sunlit, walled-in garden with sweet-scented borders. One almost stretches out one's hand to pinch a soft green leaf for the delicate aroma to linger on one's fingers. The average housewife nowadays uses her herbs for cooking. There are chives, a delicate onion substitute for salads and egg dishes; marjoram for seasonings; fennel for flavouring fish sauces; sorrel for salads and soups (the little wood sorrel leaf, too, can be used in salads). The gay marigold and nasturtium have both an important place in the herb garden, where they add a wealth of colour to the pale greens and greys of the other plants.

32

The petals of the marigold flowers are used in soups and salads and sometimes in egg dishes, while the leaves and seed of the nasturtium all add greatly to the taste of a salad.

There is also tarragon: an infusion of these delicate leaves in vinegar makes a simple salad dressing.

Most people grow sage in their garden, one of the ingredients of "mixed herbs," and balm, which is lovely to have for its sweet lemon scent. A few young balm leaves give an unusual flavour to a salad.

Do you ever have cold mint tea or mint lemonade? Both are deliciously refreshing drinks; they make a nice change and are easy to make.

When writing about herbs, I think I should tell you about bay leaves. The bay is, of course, a tree, but a couple of its dried leaves added to a little bunch of other herbs are often used to flavour stews and rice or macaroni dishes.

The drying of herbs is a very simple process, but has to be done carefully. The most usual herbs to dry for winter use are parsley, mint, thyme, sage and marjoram. With the exception of parsley, the leaves or petals must never be exposed to a scorching sun or dried in a hot oven. The process must be slow, to retain the flavour of the herb. Gather the herbs just before they flower, and, after washing them and shaking them as dry as possible, lay them on pieces of muslin to dry in the sun; or, if you prefer it, lay them on a baking sheet in your oven, which should be only moderately warm. Parsley, however, has to be dried very quickly; but be careful, it scorches easily. Marigold petals can also be dried, but this must be done in the shade. When the herbs are dry, the leaves will easily separate from their stalks and can be rubbed through a sieve.

The four herbs which go to make up a *bouquet garni* are parsley, thyme, marjoram and sage. The proportions you should use are roughly 4 tablespoons of parsley to one of thyme, one of marjoram and one of sage. When this mixture is ready, you can fill little jars with it, cover them with grease-proof paper, and label them neatly and prettily. A little jar like this makes a delightful present for any friend who has no garden of her own.

CHAPTER VIII

The Salad Bowl

"Though all th' Inhabitants of Sea and Air
Be listed in the Glutton's bill of Fare;
Yet still the Fruits of Earth we see
Plac'd the Third Story high in all her Luxury."
ABRAHAM COWLEY (1618–67) : *The Garden*

THE French are especially famous for their salads, and in many families the mixing of the salad is a ritual each day at dinner-time, the father mixing the dressing with great care and precision at the table. A very delightful book is Willa Cather's *Shadows on the Rock*, from which you get an excellent idea of how clever the French have always been with regard to food and its preparation, and how, even in those days, away back in the seventeenth century, the salad was regarded as an essential part of the diet. Miss Cather describes how in Quebec, where the climate is so terribly cold in winter, the settlers were able to buy in October rooted lettuce plants in boxes of earth, which they stored in their cellars and, carefully tending these plants, were able to serve a salad sometimes as late in the winter as January.

There are so many ways of making a salad and we have now learnt to use what at one time seemed a strange mixture. To arrange a salad prettily, especially when it is the season for some bright ingredient, is rather like arranging a vase of flowers. You can feel really flattered when someone on coming to the table, exclaims, "Oh what a pretty salad!" Raw grated vegetables often add

both to the taste and good looks of the bowl; and in America they love to mix fruit with the vegetables. But let us start with two simple salads, one for summer and the other for winter. Later you can embellish them to your own original taste with fresh fruit, cooked prunes or raisins, ground nuts, cream cheese, or some of the herbs you already know about.

I have given you a recipe for French Dressing, but until olive oil comes back into the shops you will have to use Salad Cream, either bought or home-made by your mother's recipe.

SUMMER SALAD
(Allow 25 minutes)

Ingredients	Utensils
1 large lettuce or 2 small ones.	Sharp knife.
4 tomatoes.	Pair of scissors.
1 egg.	Clean dish.
1 cucumber.	Towel.
A few chives.	Small saucepan.
	Wooden spoon and fork.
	Salad bowl.

1. Fill the saucepan with hot water and bring it to the boil. Put in the egg.
2. Cover and let boil for 10 minutes (you can be going on with the rest of the salad).
3. Pull the lettuce leaves apart and wash them well in cold water.
4. Shake them and pat them dry with your clean towel. Don't leave any drops of water on them if you can help it.
5. *Tear* the larger leaves into two or three pieces and lay all the lettuce in your salad bowl. (This is one of the few times when you don't use your kitchen scissors.)
6. Peel your cucumber (don't cut the rind too thick, as that is wasteful, but do get off all the green, as it has a bitter taste).
7. Slice the cucumber thinly on to the lettuce.

36

8. Slice the tomatoes and add them to the lettuce and cucumber.

9. Now, if the egg has boiled for 10 minutes, it is done.

10. Take the 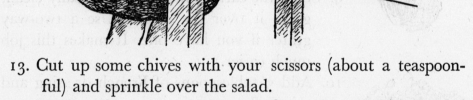 saucepan from the stove (don't forget to turn off the heat).

11. Pour off the hot water and let cold water run over the egg until it is cool. (This makes peeling easier and also gets the egg ready for your salad more quickly.)

12. Peel the shell off, and, when the egg is stone cold, slice it into the salad.

13. Cut up some chives with your scissors (about a teaspoonful) and sprinkle over the salad.

14. Lastly, add 2 or 3 tablespoons of your French dressing and mix the salad gently together.

WINTER SALAD

(Allow 25 minutes)

Ingredients	Utensils
1 large cooked beetroot.	Pair of scissors.
1 basket of mustard and	Sharp knife.
1 basket of cress.	Grater.
1 large head of celery.	Wooden spoon and fork.
1 carrot.	Salad bowl.

1. Take the skin off the beetroot, just rub it—it will slip off quite easily.

2. Cut the beetroot into thin slices and cut the slices in half if they look big or clumsy.

3. Put them in the salad bowl.

4. Lift the mustard and cress out of their baskets and cut off the seeds at the roots with your scissors.

5. Wash them if they look dirty and shake them dry, and add to the beetroot.

6. Cut off the base of the celery.

7. Pull the celery apart and wash very well, scrubbing with the vegetable brush to get the earth out of the inner curves. Don't use the really tough outside stalks for the salad.

8. Cut the clean stalks into pieces about $\frac{1}{2}$ inch long, and put in a few of the most tender leaves too.

9. Scrub the carrot and, when it is really clean, grate it over the salad. (Use a two-way grater if you have one. It makes this job much easier.)

10. Add 3 tablespoons of French dressing and mix well.

FRENCH DRESSING
(Allow 15 minutes)

Ingredients	Utensils
6 tablespoons olive oil.	Glass jar with a screw-
3 tablespoons vinegar.	on lid or a wide-
$\frac{1}{4}$ teaspoon pepper.	mouthed bottle
1 saltspoon sugar.	with a tight cork.
$\frac{1}{2}$ teaspoon salt.	Tablespoon.
	Saltspoon. Teaspoon.

1. Put everything together in the jar or bottle.
2. Cover tightly, shake well.

This will keep without spoiling for several weeks in a cool place. Use 3 tablespoons of the dressing or more on your salad. Turn the salad in the bowl over and over with the wooden spoon and fork after you have added the dressing. Do it gently, so that you don't bruise the lettuce leaves, but thoroughly, to make sure that every leaf and slice of vegetable is well coated.

CHAPTER IX

A Friend to Tea

YOU'VE had a tea party for your sister's dolls, and you've got tea for your mother, but now wouldn't it be fun to have someone just your own age for tea? Your best friend at school, perhaps? Choose an afternoon when you can have the kitchen for about an hour before tea, so that you can get it all ready by yourself. What will you have? You could just put the loaf and the butter

and jam on the table, but sandwiches would make it seem more of a party. So why not have jam sandwiches, and, if it's the summer time, a few made with tomato? And, of course, cake. Little cakes made in patty pans are pretty, especially if you have some paper doilies to lay on the plate under them.

I should make the cakes first, then while they are baking you can be getting on with the sandwiches. But don't forget that your cakes are in the oven!

And after you have had your tea, how about washing up? I'm sure your friend would help, and it's no bother at all—in fact, it's fun when the two of you do it together.

The next time she comes to tea, why not ask her to come and help make the cakes with you first?

CAKE
(Allow 1 hour)

Ingredients	*Utensils*
4 oz. margarine.	2 mixing basins.
3 oz. granulated sugar.	Scales.
1 egg, fresh or dried.	Tablespoon, teaspoon, knife.
6 tablespoons milk.	Small basin.
6 oz. self-raising flour.	Fine sieve.
$\frac{1}{2}$ teaspoon vanilla essence.	Egg whisk.
$\frac{1}{4}$ teaspoon salt.	12 patty pans.
Lard for greasing the pan.	Small piece of greaseproof paper.
	Wooden spoon.

1. Light the oven; set it at "hot."
2. Put the margarine into a mixing basin. Cut it into three or four pieces and let it stand while you grease your patty pans.
3. Put a tiny piece of lard on the small piece of greaseproof paper and rub round the inside of the patty pans. Be sure they are all well greased, down in the corners and all, and then put a pinch of flour in each one and give it a shake so

the inside is dusted with flour. This will make your cakes come out of the pans easily when they are cooked.

4. Now stir and smash your margarine in the mixing basin until it is soft and creamy.

5. Add half the sugar and stir again.

6. Break the egg into the small basin and whisk it with the rest of the sugar. (If you are using dried egg powder, follow the directions on the packet for mixing it with water to "reconstitute".)

7. Add to the margarine and sugar mixture. The batter may look curdled, but this is nothing to worry about.

8. Sift the flour and salt together into the other mixing basin.

9. Add a little flour at a time to the first mixture, first a little flour and then a little milk, keeping the batter smooth and the same thickness until all the milk and flour are used up.

10. Add the vanilla.

11. Don't go on beating once the cake is mixed.

12. Put a spoonful of batter into each patty pan, filling them about two-thirds full.

13. Bake 25 minutes.

14. Don't keep opening the oven door to see how the cakes are getting on. Look at the end of 15 minutes, but not before, and then open the oven door very gently and shut it carefully so your cakes won't fall.

16. To see if the cake is done: Take a straw from the top of the broom. *Wash* it and dry it and run it into the middle of a cake. If it comes out clean, the cake is done, if it comes out with a little dough still on it, the cake is not quite cooked. (A thin knitting needle can be used for this instead of a straw.)

17. You can be washing up while the cake is cooking, and if the floor has flour sifted on to it wipe it up.

18. When you take your cake out, leave the pans standing on the kitchen table for 5 minutes, but not in a draught, and then loosen the cakes with a round-ended knife. Then wait a minute or two and you'll be able to lift the little cakes out easily.

SANDWICHES
(Allow 30 minutes)

Ingredients	*Utensils*
2–4 oz. margarine.	Sharp bread knife and bread board.
3 firm tomatoes.	Table knife.
Some jam.	Sharp little vegetable knife.
A loaf of bread. (Don't use new bread; it crumbles when you cut it. Better use a loaf that is a day old.)	Sheet of white paper or greaseproof. Medium basin. Wooden spoon.

1. Put the margarine in the basin and smash it and stir it with the wooden spoon until it is soft and creamy.

43

2. Cut 8 slices of bread and keep them in order so they will fit each other.

3. Lay them out on your sheet of white paper. Keep them in order so they will fit when you want to put them together in pairs.

4. Spread the butter evenly on each slice.

5. Slice your tomatoes as thinly as you can.

6. Lay them on two slices of bread.

7. Put the other buttered piece of bread on top. Now cut the sandwiches in half.

8. Make the jam sandwiches the same way.

CHAPTER X

French Vegetable Soup

"Beautiful Soup, so rich and green
Waiting in a hot tureen!
Who for such dainties would not stoop?
Soup of the evening, beautiful Soup!

*   *   *   *

Beautiful Soup! Who cares for fish,
Game, or any other dish?
Who would not give all else for twop
ennyworth only of beautiful Soup?"
LEWIS CARROLL: *Alice in Wonderland*

SOUP is one of the important dishes to learn about in the kitchen, especially as it can often be prepared beforehand and then just warmed up when needed. When you are learning to cook, this is a great help, because it is difficult for a beginner to manage the preparation of more than one dish or course at a time.

If you were a French girl, you would probably have a steaming hot bowl of soup given you on most evenings for your supper. There's many a good vegetable soup made in French kitchens each week, soups that don't even need meat or fish stock (water in which meat or fish has been cooked) or milk as a base, but are simply made of fresh vegetables cooked in plain water. A good country soup can be very nourishing, and there are so many variations that there is no fear of boring your family with it. In fact, a really expert cook prides herself on being able to make her soups from almost anything there is handy in the larder. Here those herbs come in as flavourings, and then the garnishings—how they add to a soup! I am sure

45

you like fried *croutons*, or little cheese straws, just to mention two out of quite a number.

Here, then, is a recipe for one of these "peasant" soups. It is a simple one, but when you've made it and it is all ready to serve, you will get much pride from the little tray on which stand perhaps four bowls of piping hot soup, each bowl sending up its little curly wreath of smoky steam.

FRENCH VEGETABLE SOUP

(Allow 1 hour)

Ingredients	Utensils
1 carrot.	Vegetable scrubbing brush.
1 onion.	Small sharp knife and a board for cutting.
A few stalks of celery.	
1 potato.	*Or* a chopping bowl and chopper.
1 turnip.	
Quarter of a head of cabbage.	Medium-size saucepan.
1 tablespoon bacon fat or dripping.	Wooden spoon.
	Serving bowl or casserole.
1 dessertspoon Marmite or beef extract.	
3 tablespoons grated cheese.	

1. Scrub the carrot and the celery.
2. Peel the potato and the turnip.
3. Peel the onion.

4. Cut all these vegetables into small pieces with your sharp knife on the board or chop them fine in the chopping bowl

with the chopper. (After you have finished cutting up the onion, you can get rid of the smell on your hands and the knife by rubbing them with salt and washing them in cold water.)

5. Put the cut-up vegetables (not the cabbage—that comes later) into the saucepan with the fat or dripping.

6. Fry very gently for ten minutes, moving about with the wooden spoon.

7. Add 2 pints of cold water and bring to the boil.

8. Simmer gently until the vegetables are soft (about 20 minutes).

9. Stir in the beef extract and stir until it is dissolved.

10. See that the cabbage is clean and cut it into fine shreds, and add to the soup.

11. Boil for 2 minutes and pour into your serving bowl.

12. Sprinkle the grated cheese on the top and serve.

CROUTONS

(Allow 15 minutes)

Ingredients	Utensils
2 slices of bread.	Bread board and bread knife.
2 dessertspoons dripping or bacon fat.	Frying pan. Wooden spoon.

1. Cut the bread into little cubes about the size of the end of your thumb.

2. Put the fat in the frying pan and let it get hot. (Piping hot, otherwise the bread just won't get crisp, no matter how long you cook it.)

3. Put in the little pieces of bread.

4. Cook over a medium fire, stirring all the time, until the bread is brown and crisp.

5. Serve in a separate bowl along with the hot soup.

CHAPTER XI

Stew in Oven, Semolina Pudding

YOU know what happens when one of those comfortable-looking earthenware dishes is placed in front of your father and he takes off the lid? There's a tiny pause and everyone —they just can't help it—imperceptibly sniffs and then relaxes.

It's just too good for words—Mother's best and most tasty stew, when you are all so hungry!

You could make a good stew, too, and I think you should try. It's a dish that can be cooked in the oven, so what about making a semolina pudding at the same time and so completing a meal?

The semolina pudding is easy: the stew is more complicated,

but well within your range, and I am glad to say needs some of your herb knowledge to make it really delicious. You have to make a start on the cooking of fresh meat some time, and preparing meat for a stew is very simple.

Ask your mother to get the butcher to cut the beef into $1\frac{1}{2}$-inch cubes, or do it for you herself. The rest you can do all alone.

OVEN STEW

(Allow $\frac{1}{2}$ hour for preparing and $3\frac{1}{2}$ hours for cooking—
4 hours in all)

8/1/59.

Ingredients	Utensils
1 pound of stewing steak.	Big kitchen knife and the cutting
1 onion.	board.
4 potatoes, medium size.	Big casserole.
2 carrots.	Frying pan.
$\frac{1}{2}$ teaspoon salt.	Sharp knife.
$\frac{1}{4}$ teaspoon pepper.	Vegetable brush.
$\frac{3}{4}$ pint hot water.	The scales.
1 oz. dripping or bacon	A wooden spoon.
fat.	Pint measure.
1 Bay leaf.	
1 oz. margarine.	
2 oz. plain flour.	
Gravy colouring.	

1. Light your oven and set it to "slow."
2. Put the dripping or bacon fat into the frying pan and heat gently.
3. Put in the pieces of meat and fry for 5 minutes until the meat is browned.
4. Put into the casserole with the salt, the pepper, and the hot water.
5. Cover the casserole and put it in the oven.
6. Scrub the carrots well and scrape them if they are very tough and dirty on the outside.
7. Cut them into thin slices.
8. Peel the onions and cut into slices.

50

9. Scrub your potatoes, peel them, and cut them in quarters.
10. Let your beef cook for 2 hours in the oven and then add the vegetables and bay leaf. Stir well.
11. Cook for another hour.
12. Cream the margarine until it is soft and add the flour. Mix well.
13. Take your casserole out of the oven and set it on the table (on an asbestos mat).
14. Take off the lid and stir in your margarine and flour mixture. Stir it well and put it back into the oven for another ½ hour.
15. Darken it by stirring in about 1 teaspoonful of gravy colouring.

SEMOLINA PUDDING
(Allow 1 hour)

Ingredients	Utensils
4½ level tablespoons semolina.	Medium size basin.
1 level tablespoon sugar.	Tablespoon.
1 pinch of salt.	Pint measure.
1½ pints of milk.	Double saucepan.
Grated nutmeg.	Pie dish.

1. Mix the semolina, sugar and salt in the basin with a little of the cold milk.
2. Bring the rest of the milk to boil in the top part of the double saucepan and pour it on the blended semolina.
3. Mix it well and put it back in the saucepan, directly over the flame.
4. Stir it until it boils.
5. And then let it cook over boiling water (which is in the lower part of the double saucepan) for 15 minutes.
6. Pour into a pie dish and grate a little nutmeg on top.
7. Bake in a medium oven for about ½ hour till it has a nice brown skin on the top.

CHAPTER XII

Sunday Supper

I USED to love doing a surprise for my mother. Sometimes it would be a very simple surprise, like a bowl of flowers in her bedroom, and sometimes it would be more complicated, like getting a meal, and then I would have to let my father into the

secret so he could help arrange it. You might get supper for your mother one Sunday night. This means that you have to start thinking about it on Saturday morning, to be sure that you will have everything you need when you come to prepare the meal. So decide what you are going to have, and make a list of what to get.

Suppose you choose a menu something like this:

Cold meat.
Salad.
Baked potatoes.
Jelly and cakes.

Perhaps there is some meat from the roast left, and that would do for supper, but if there isn't any, then you could buy at the shop some cold sliced sausage, or you could cook a pound of sausages the day before or in the morning and let them get cold. Look at the recipe for salad, and be sure you have all those ingredients. The baked potato recipe is an old friend. Just count up how many potatoes you will need and see that there are enough in the larder. For the jelly you need a bottle of lemon or orange squash and some powdered gelatine. Cakes—is there flour, baking powder and so forth in the store cupboard?

Now when you have all the provisions for supper, you must plan the time you'll need as well. The cold meat or the sausages you can see to in the morning of the day before. And I should get the cakes and the jelly made ahead of time too. That leaves you just the potatoes and the salad to do on Sunday night.

Allow yourself plenty of time to do a meal like this. Work out a time-table backwards. Supposing you want to have supper on the table at seven o'clock; the potatoes ought to go into a hot oven forty minutes before that, which would be twenty minutes past six. Better say 6.15, just to be on the safe side. That means you'll be starting to scrub them at six. While the potatoes are cooking, you can be making the salad, so, if you are going to lay the table for this meal, you had better get that done and finished with before six. How long does it take you? Half an hour? That brings you back to half-past five, so it seems that five o'clock would be a good time to start getting everything ready in the kitchen, slicing the meat, arranging it on a dish (a little parsley makes it look professional), setting the cakes on a plate and turning out your jelly.

53

The best plan of all is to write down a schedule for yourself like this:

5 o'clock to 6 o'clock. Arrange food that is already cooked and lay the table.

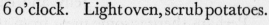

6 o'clock.   Light oven, scrub potatoes.

6.15.   Put potatoes into the oven and make salad.

6.45.   Put everything on the table and go and wash your face and brush your hair. (You have no idea how untidy you can get after two hours in the kitchen. And it's very clever to serve up the meal looking as smooth as silk.)

6.55.   Take the potatoes out of oven and call the family.

7 o'clock.   Supper.

Now you have got a whole meal and are a cook!

SAUSAGES
(Allow 30 minutes)

Ingredients	Utensils
1 lb. sausages	Scissors.
	Fork.
1 dessertspoon dripping.	The oven.
	A shallow baking tin.

1. Light the oven.
2. Cut the sausages apart with the scissors and lay them in a shallow baking tin.
3. Prick each one with a fork.

4. Put in a medium oven and cook for 20 minutes or $\frac{1}{2}$ hour, until the skins are crisp and brown.

You can also fry them in a frying pan; it is quicker to cook them in the frying pan, but they are more apt to split apart than when they are cooked in the oven.

SQUASH JELLY

(Allow 10 minutes for making, 2 hours for setting)

Ingredients	*Utensils*
1 pint of orange or lemon or grapefruit squash.	Saucepan.
	Tablespoon.
1 oz. granulated gelatine.	Basin that will hold a little
4 tablespoons cold water.	more than a pint (or a jelly mould).
	Breakfast cup.

1. Put the gelatine into the breakfast cup with the cold water.
2. Put the squash into the saucepan and bring it to the boil.
3. Take it off the fire and add the soaked gelatine.
4. Stir until the gelatine is dissolved.
5. Fill the basin or mould with cold water and pour it out, and don't dry the inside of it. Pour the hot jelly into the wet basin and leave it to set in a cool place (the shelf in the larder). It will take at least 2 hours to

55

set, so it is a good plan to make this in the morning or the day before you want to use it.

6. To turn it out of the basin or mould: dip a tea towel in hot water and hold it round the outside of the basin or mould and then put your serving dish or platter on the top of the basin. With a quick flip of your wrist, turn the whole thing upside down and the jelly should come out with a little plop. You lift up the basin and there sits the jelly in the middle of the dish.

CHAPTER XIII

Pastry

"The Queen of Hearts
She made some tarts . . ."

PASTRY-MAKING, even if it is a bit messy until you get really good at it, is fun, and when you hear your mother saying to a friend, "She really has a very light hand for pastry," then you can feel proud.

There are many ways of using pastry, both as sweets and savouries. To start with, there are the little tarts that the Knave stole, which can be filled with jam or fruit or some custard mixture; a large, round, flat open tart can have the same kind of filling or it can be filled with mixed vegetables in a cheese sauce and covered with pastry; then there is the famous English fruit tart (or pie, as it is called in the North)—a deep dish filled with sweet, juicy fruit and topped with your best light pastry. Mince pies at Christmas everyone in Britain knows, and the little cheese straws to go with soup are made from pastry. All these dishes are equally good hot or cold, and that is helpful for a beginner who may want to prepare one of her main courses beforehand.

There are several ways of making pastry, depending how you rub the fat into the flour, but the recipe in this section for short crust pastry is the one I think you will find most useful.

57

JAM TARTS

(Allow 45 minutes)

Ingredients	Utensils
8 oz. plain flour.	Scales.
½ teaspoon salt.	Medium to
2 oz. lard.	large basin.
2 oz. margarine.	Sieve.
Cold water.	Knife.
Jam.	Tablespoon.
	Teaspoon.

Rolling pin and pastry board (or you can use the top of the kitchen table).
Scone-cutters or the top of a tumbler.
Patty pans.

The whole secret of making good pastry is to get as much air into the flour as you can and to keep it there. This takes time and patience; it's no good rushing at it and banging it about. You have to work slowly and lightly, a little bit at a time.

1. Sift the flour and salt into the basin.
2. Cut the margarine and lard into little pieces, about as big as the end of your thumb, and add them to the flour.
3. With the very tips of your fingers, rub

58

the fat into the flour, lifting the flour up as you go along and letting it crumble back into the bowl. Keep doing this very gently, being sure that you are not neglecting the flour at the bottom of the basin; reach under and lift it up, letting it fall through your fingers from time to time.

4. When there are no more little lumps of fat to be seen, when the whole mixture looks like fine breadcrumbs, you are finished. But it will take 5 minutes at least, and don't hurry.

5. Wash your hands.

6. Now add the cold water 1 tablespoon at a time and cut into the flour with a knife. Don't stir with a spoon. Go slowly with the water, being sure each lot is well cut in before you add the next. I can't tell you exactly how much water to use, but you must stop as soon as the dough is damp enough so that it all sticks together and you can make one soft round ball of it, with nothing left on the side of the basin.

7. Put 1 spoonful of flour on the pastry board or the table top (it's clean, of course) and rub a little flour on to the rolling pin.

8. Put your ball of dough on to the flour and pat it out with your hands.

9. Roll out the dough flat, but with very light gentle strokes of the rolling pin. Always push the rolling pin away from you, and turn the piece of dough a little after each stroke so that it becomes a nice, evenly shaped flat circle. Don't press down hard with the rolling pin, will you?

10. When the dough is about $\frac{1}{4}$ inch thick, cut out rounds

with the scone-cutter or the top of the tumbler. It's a good plan to dip the cutter into a little heap of flour first, then the dough won't stick to it.

11. Lift your little cut-out circles into the patty pans, fitting them in nicely.

12. Gather up all the odd bits of dough into one piece and roll out again (gently) and cut more circles.

13. Repeat until there is no more dough left. The last bit you'll have to just shape as best you can; it will be a bit uneven, but fine to eat as soon as it is done.

14. Put a small spoonful of jam in each pastry circle.

15. Cook on the top shelf of the oven for 20 minutes. It may take less time; better look at them from time to time and take them out when they are golden brown.

16. That last little bit of pastry that made such an uneven circle will do very well to try to see how your pastry has come out, won't it? I hope it's a great success.

CHAPTER XIV

Cauliflower Cheese

"A Frenchman once said: '*On devient cuisinier, on devient rotisseur, on est ne saucier.*' ('You can become a cook and learn to roast, but you can only be born a maker of sauces.') The old definition of genius—'an infinite capacity for taking pains'—will make a 'Saucerer.' "

MRS. LEYEL and MISS HARTLEY: *The Gentle Art of Cookery*

BY this you will see that it takes a really good cook to make a white sauce, but that the most important factor in the making of a sauce is "care." You must stand by your sauce, keeping a sharp eye on it to see that it does not get too hot, then boil and spoil. If you can learn to make the perfect plain sauce (it must *not* be just good, but perfect, mind!), you can then make many different sauces, as the main differences lie in their flavourings.

It would be sensible to start with a dish which can be served as a course on its own, so I suggest "cauliflower cheese." It is a straightforward one to make, because, apart from the sauce which makes the dish, there is only the vegetable to cook, and that you will find quite simple to do. Why, if you can make a dish like this and find some fresh or stewed fruit or cake in the larder, you can make coffee, and there's a complete meal.

WHITE SAUCE
(Allow 25 minutes)

Ingredients	*Utensils*
2 level tablespoons margarine.	2 medium-size saucepans.
2 level tablespoons plain flour.	Wooden spoon.
½ pint of milk.	Tablespoon.
½ teaspoon salt.	Teaspoon
Few grains pepper.	Pint measure.

1. Put the margarine into a saucepan and melt it over a gentle heat.

2. Add the flour and mix well. Keep it over the heat for 2 minutes, stirring all the time.

3. Put the milk in the other saucepan and bring it to the boil.

4. Tip it back into the measure (it will be easier to pour).

5. Now put the margarine and flour back on the heat and add the milk, very gradually stirring all the time. Don't pour the milk in a steady stream, stop from time to time and stir, so as to keep the sauce smooth and free from lumps.

6. Add the salt and pepper.

If (in spite of you being awfully careful) the sauce *has* lumped, then all you do is rub it through a sieve into the other saucepan, the one you heated the milk in, and no harm done.

CAULIFLOWER CHEESE
(Allow 45–50 minutes)

Ingredients	*Utensils*
1 large cauliflower.	Large saucepan.
1 level teaspoon salt.	Large kitchen knife.
¼–½ lb. cheese, a few days old, not	Casserole.
fresh and crumbly.	Grater.

1. With the kitchen knife, take off the lower part of the cauliflower's stalk and the thick outside leaves, but leave on the little tender pale-green leaves.

2. Put enough water in the saucepan so that the cauliflower will be covered (but don't put the cauliflower in yet) and set it on the stove and bring to the boil.

3. Now wash the cauliflower well in cold water. A very good plan is to fill the sink or a big basin with cold water and add a table-spoonful of salt and soak the cauliflower in, the head down for a few minutes. If there are any garden slugs or caterpillars lurking inside, they will come out and then you won't be overcome with shame at the table.

4. If the cauliflower is too big to go into the pot comfortably, break it into two or three pieces.

5. When the water boils, add the teaspoonful of salt and then the cauli- flower. Put the lid on and boil gently from 20 to 30 minutes.

6. Test it with a fork, and if it feels soft it is done. Take off the stove and pour the water away. Does your mother keep vegetable water for soup?

7. Lay the cauliflower in the casserole.

8. While it is cooking, make your white sauce.

9. Grate the cheese and add it to the white sauce. Stir well and pour it over the cauliflower in the casserole. Slip it into a hot oven for 5 minutes or under the grill till it is golden brown on top.

10. Serve.

CHAPTER XV

Another Dish with White Sauce

"We will dine on a fish more tasty than any bearded mullet that ever floundered in the porphyry fishponds of the new rich at Baiæ: a noble monster, with succulent flakes as pink as rosebuds, netted by coracle-fishers in the foamy stickles of clear Sabrina this very day. The salmon, we call it."

FRANCIS BRETT YOUNG: *The Island.*

PRACTICE is very necessary for the sauce-maker, so let's try salmon served with a white sauce and with buttered crumbs on top. (This is the first time you have used fish, which is perhaps one of the most difficult foods to handle.) But you don't need fresh salmon for this; a tin of good salmon will do very well, and will be all ready for use, which will help you a great deal.

All fish is very nourishing, and salmon especially so. For centuries now

64

fishermen have caught it in our rivers and realised its good qualities. A Roman centurion, settled in England, spoke the lines I've quoted above to his guest, another Roman centurion who had just arrived from Rome as long ago as A.D. 78.

SALMON IN WHITE SAUCE WITH BUTTERED CRUMBS
(Allow 50 minutes)

Ingredients	Utensils
1 large tin of salmon.	Casserole.
Recipe for white sauce.	Frying pan.
3 slices of bread.	Wooden spoon.
2 oz. margarine.	

1. Make the white sauce and leave it in the saucepan.
2. Open the tin of salmon, or ask your mother to do it for you.
3. Add the salmon to the white sauce in the saucepan and mix well together.
4. Light the oven and set it to "medium."
5. Melt the margarine in the frying pan.
6. Crumble the soft part of the bread into very small crumbs.
7. Add them to the melted margarine in the frying pan and stir them about.
8. See that they are all well mixed with the margarine.
9. Put the salmon and white sauce mixture into the casserole.
10. Put the crumbs on the top; spread over as evenly as you can.
11. Put the casserole in the oven and bake for 20 minutes or until the crumbs begin to brown on top.
12. You could be washing up the saucepans and frying pan while it's in the oven, couldn't you?

CHAPTER XVI

The Lighter Side of Cooking—Fudge

YOU can buy all sorts of sweets to hand round after your tea party, but it would be much nicer to make some of your own. They can be made any time when the kitchen is free, so you need not be in anyone's way when you try out your first experiment.

It is possible that you will find you've made more than you need for this one occasion. If so, here is another idea for a present. All you need are pieces of coloured paper, roughly 10 inches square, and some gay ribbon. Tumble about a dozen pieces of your fudge into the centre of the square, pick up the four corners of the paper to a peak above the sweets and tie a piece of ribbon round the paper so as to make a knobbly cushion at the bottom.

Then carefully spread out the four corners of the paper above the ribbon to give a flower-like effect.

If you like, you can take smaller pieces of paper and fill them with just three or four sweets and put them by your visitors' places at tea. This makes the table look very gay. And don't forget, little packets like this can be hung on the Christmas tree with great effect. Once you've made fudge, you'll go on to the making of other sweets, I feel sure.

FUDGE
(Allow 30–45 minutes)

Ingredients	Utensils
5½ level tablespoons cocoa.	Large saucepan.
3 level tablespoons margarine.	Wooden spoon.
1 lb. granulated sugar.	Tablespoon.
1 tablespoon golden syrup.	Pint measure.
Pinch of salt.	Scales.
6 oz. (12 tablespoons) milk.	Teaspoon.
1 teaspoon Vanilla.	Sandwich tin.
	Glass of water.

1. Keep back 2 tablespoons margarine and put all the rest of the ingredients in the saucepan.

2. Stir constantly over a medium heat until the sugar has dissolved and the mixture boils.

3. Put a lid on your saucepan and boil 3 minutes (don't turn the flame too high; just keep it boiling).

4. Take the lid off and boil, stirring occasionally.

5. While the fudge is boiling, rub the sandwich tin well with margarine, as though you were greasing it for a cake.

6. Keep the fudge boiling until it reaches the "soft ball" stage. This means that when you drop a little bit of the hot fudge into a glass of cold water, you will see the fudge form a

soft mass. You can reach down into the water with your hand and roll the little ball of fudge between your fingers. It probably won't be firm enough the first time you test it. Keep on trying until you can make a soft little ball between your thumb and fingers.

7. Then take the saucepan off the stove and leave the fudge in it to get lukewarm (when the pan feels just warm to the touch, the fudge inside is right).

8. Add the other 2 tablespoons of margarine and beat the fudge with your wooden spoon for a minute or so until you can feel the fudge thickening.

9. Stir in the vanilla.

10. Pour the fudge into your greased sandwich tin and leave in a cool place to set.

11. When it is firm, cut it into squares. You can make tidy pieces if you dip the knife you are cutting with into hot water from time to time as you make the squares.

This recipe, like the one for French Dressing, may have to wait until scarce foods are more plentiful.

CHAPTER XVII

Blackberry Jam

"Here, concentrated in this lustrous purple pot,
Are speckled autumn days not easily forgot,
Hedges of graceful fruiting bramble sprays,
Arching the dry and crumbling brown pathways.
Spill out the jelly on to fresh-made bread
And taste this coloured warmth the sun has shed."

A. G.

IF you want to make blackberry jam, you will have to organise your family and go blackberrying one fine day when the fruit is nice and dry. Blackberrying in a party is great fun; if the hedges are near home, you may go out in the afternoon, pick hard until you have the amount of fruit required, and then return home to a well-earned tea, feeling virtuous after all your work. If, however, you live some distance from the best black-berries—in a town, perhaps—here's a good excuse for a picnic.

Don't be impatient to go too early in the season; it is so much easier and quicker to pick when the fruit is abundant and each berry is large and luscious. There will probably be some rivalry as to who has picked the most fruit, so each person should have his basket or tin. Ask each picker to take care to pick only the good berries—this is very easy at the height of the season when the sprays are heavily weighted with fruit—and not to put in their baskets the small, "woody" berries. If everyone does this, you will find the task of cleaning the fruit before you start jam-making very much quicker and easier.

There is something really exciting about jam-making—it's going to look so lovely in the jars, and a little jar with an extra pretty label on it, and perhaps a jaunty ribbon tied round its neck, makes the

69

nicest present for a friend who hasn't been able to get to those blackberries herself.

BLACKBERRY JAM
(Allow 45 minutes or 1 hour)

Ingredients	Utensils
1 lb. blackberries.	Large saucepan.
¾ lb. sugar.	Scales.
	Basin.
	Wooden spoon.
	Teaspoon.
	Saucer.
	2 1-lb. jam jars.

1. Wash the jam jars well in hot soapy water, rinse, dry and set aside.
2. Light the oven and set it to "low."
3. Pick over the blackberries and take out any bad ones or dirty ones or any little wandering animals.
4. Weigh the fruit and then put it into the saucepan.

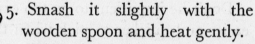

5. Smash it slightly with the wooden spoon and heat gently.
6. Weigh the sugar and put it in the basin in the oven to warm.
7. When the juice begins to run from the fruit and the sugar is warm, add the sugar to the fruit and stir until the sugar is dissolved.
8. Bring it quickly up to the boiling point.
9. Let it boil hard until the setting point is reached. This means that when you take up a spoonful and let the jam drip and fall back into the saucepan the juice is a little thicker and more syrupy than it was. Then with a teaspoon put a few drops on to the saucer and set it in

the window or away from the stove. In a minute, when the little sample is cool, touch it with your finger. If it has a little skin over it, if it holds together well and is more than syrupy, but not absolutely set in a stiff jelly, then your jam is done.

10. Take the saucepan off the stove and let the jam cool before you pour it out. Then, using a teacup or a little jug or a good big ladle, pour the jam into the jam jars. Fill one right up and the other one as far as you have jam for (probably not to the top).

11. Cover the full jar with cellophane, following the directions on the packet. Or let the jam get cool and pour melted candle wax over the top to make a little roof. Write a label and paste it on the jar; date, etc. The other pot, the one that is half-full, you can serve to your family for tea or breakfast. I'm sure they'll be anxious to try your jam right away.

CHAPTER VIII

A Picnic

"A little bit of bread and no cheese."
Yellowhammer's song

WELL, if you are going to ask your friends to help you pick blackberries, you'll have to provide picnic food for them. Let's hustle round the kitchen and see what there is. It's a golden rule to take more food than you think you'll need on a picnic; you'll find that hardly anything comes back, as, somehow, everyone wants to eat enormously out in the fresh air.

There's always the hard-boiled egg, but why not be more interesting and prepare stuffed eggs? They make a change, and your guests will be duly impressed when they undo the twists of greaseproof paper and find this delicious preparation inside. I am sure they will find them so good that each person will want a "second," so I hope there will be enough eggs in the kitchen! This recipe is one you can easily follow:

STUFFED EGGS

(Allow 25 minutes)

Ingredients

As many hard-boiled eggs as there are people in your picnic.
½ teaspoon of melted margarine for each egg.
Salt and pepper to taste.
Or, ½ teaspoon salad cream or ½ teaspoon French dressing for each egg.

1. Hard boil the eggs (see recipe in the chapter on salads, p. 36).
2. When they are peeled, cut the eggs in half lengthways, scoop the yolks out carefully without breaking the whites, and put them in a basin.
3. Mash them with a fork and add a little melted margarine, and season to taste. Or salad cream or French dressing, enough to moisten the yolks and make a nice creamy mixture.
4. With a teaspoon, put the filling back into the white and put the two halves together again.

5. Lay each egg on a square of greaseproof paper, wrap them up and twist the ends.

Sandwiches, of course, for a picnic. Some to eat with the stuffed eggs and plenty to eat separately.

The great art of sandwich making is the careful cutting of the bread—it should be neither too thick nor too thin—and then to be generous with your fillings.

You made sandwiches in the chapter "A Friend to Tea" (recipe, p. 43). Those were filled with jam or sliced tomatoes. Paste sandwiches are good out of doors and easy to make, and cucumber sandwiches are always good—they are moist when you are thirsty. Peel the cucumber and cut it into slices of equal thickness; sprinkle a very little salt on them before you clap on the top piece of bread.

Greaseproof paper you will need again for wrapping the sandwiches, and, if possible, rubber bands. Wrap each different kind of sandwich separately, write on the paper what the packet contains, and slip a rubber band round it. If you have no rubber bands, use thin string and tie the packets tightly.

Fruit is a refreshing dessert on a picnic, so pack whatever is available. If this is an autumn blackberrying expedition, there will be apples or pears—and perhaps a piece of chocolate for each member of the party.

Have you thought of the problem of drinks? Being out of doors always makes one thirsty, so make some of your best lemonade and put it into a couple of bottles. There won't be an unlimited quantity for each person, but a mugful is good to drink, and the fruit you had as dessert is refreshing and helps to quench the thirst too.

This picnic lunch may not sound as exotic as the one that Rat provided for Mole and himself in the *Wind in the Willows*. Do you remember it? Mole asked what was inside the fat wicker luncheon basket, and Rat replied briefly: "There's chicken inside it, coldtonguecoldhamcoldbeefpickledgurkinssaladfrenchrollscress sandwichespottedmeatgingerbeerlemonadesodawater." But I am quite sure it will be a huge success and will tempt you to organise others on fine days when the urge to follow the open road falls upon you.

CHAPTER XIX

Eggs and Bacon

LET'S come back into the house for our next kitchen adventure. It's Sunday morning and both your mother and father like that little extra lie in bed, that most grown-ups indulge in on this day of rest. It's not really a day of rest for your mother, I feel sure, for she probably has to serve up lunch, tea and supper for the family; so what about preparing breakfast yourself? Sunday-morning breakfast is one of the happiest family meals. No one is in a hurry to catch a train or get to school punctually. There is plenty of time for talk, and that second hot cup of coffee or tea can be drunk in a leisurely way—the grown-ups, perhaps, lighting cigarettes, their chairs making a scraping noise on the floor as they turn slightly round to the warm, crackly fire.

What would you think of giving them? That favourite English breakfast dish, eggs and bacon? With coffee or tea, and toast and marmalade? You know all about coffee and tea and toast, so the new recipe will be for eggs and bacon.

FRIED EGGS AND BACON
(Allow 25 minutes)

Ingredients	Utensils
Rashers of bacon (1–2 for each person).	Frying pan.
	Kitchen scissors.
Eggs (1 for each person).	Flat pancake-turner or fish slice.

76

1. Light the oven and turn it to its lowest possible heat. Put the dish or plates on which you are going to serve your bacon and eggs in the oven to be warming.

2. Cut the rind off the rashers of bacon (but don't throw them away, they are very useful for flavouring soup). Cut the rashers in two if they are very long.

3. Lay the bacon in the frying pan and fry over a medium heat, turning them from time to time. Some people like their bacon pink and limp; others prefer theirs to be crisp and brown. Better find out just how your parents want theirs. When the bacon is practically cooked, take it out of the frying pan and put it on the plate in the oven to keep warm.

4. Now, taste in fried eggs differs too. Do your parents like their eggs smooth and white on the bottom, or do they like the edges to be all frizzy and brown? If they like their fried eggs smooth, then you must let the fat in the frying pan cool before you put the eggs in, and cook the eggs over a very slow fire. But if they like them frizzed, then drop your eggs into hot fat and keep the fire at a medium heat.

5. When the white of the eggs is firm and thick, none of it runny at all, very carefully lift the eggs out with your fish slice on to the warm plates.

6. Serve.

CHAPTER XX

Five Festivals

NOW you have cooked something for every meal of the day and, what is more, you can turn out a whole meal by yourself. In this chapter let's make dishes for special occasions. We'll begin early in the year with Shrove Tuesday—that is, the Tuesday before Lent, and a day on which people in some parts of the world are very gay, dancing and making music in the streets. Here in England we generally mark Shrove Tuesday by making pancakes, and this is the recipe for them:

PANCAKES

Ingredients	Utensils
4 oz. self-raising flour.	Mixing bowl.
1 egg, fresh, or 1 tablespoon dried egg.	The scales.
	The pint jug.
A pinch of salt.	The tablespoon.
½ pint of milk or milk and water.	A wooden spoon.
	A sieve.
½ oz. dripping.	Frying pan.
2 tablespoons of sugar, the juice of a lemon or 2 tablespoons of jam.	A fish slice.
	An egg whisk.

This quantity ample for 2 folk.

1. Sift the flour and the salt and the dried egg (if you are using dried egg) all together in a mixing bowl. Make a hollow in the centre.

2. If you use a fresh egg, break it into the hollow now.

3. Pour in gradually half the milk (or milk and water) and stir it in, keeping the wall of flour as long as you can, just scraping down a little of the flour as your spoon goes round each time.

78

4. Do this until the liquid is absorbed and the liquid is smooth and creamy. Now beat with a whisk until the batter is full of air bubbles and then add the rest of the liquid. (An extra tablespoon of water if you used dried eggs.)

5. Pour all your batter into the jug.

6. Melt your dripping in the frying pan and get it smoking hot.

7. Pour just enough batter in to cover the bottom of the pan, tipping the pan so that it runs right up to each edge.

8. Cook on gentle heat till brown, flip it over either with a fish slice or, what is much more fun, by tossing the pancake in the air and catching it in the pan as it comes down.

9. Cook until brown, remove from the fire, spread with the lemon juice and sugar or with the jam and roll up.

10. Put on a warm dish and keep hot until you have cooked the whole of the batter.

Shrove Tuesday begins Lent and Easter Sunday finishes it. Have you ever hunted for Easter eggs in the long grass? Decorating Easter eggs is very simple. In the old days people used to tie the eggs up with bits of coloured cotton cloth and then drop them into boiling water. By the time the eggs were hard-boiled, the dye had run out of the cloth and given the eggs a pretty marble effect. Nowadays the colours in most cotton cloth don't run—not even in boiling water, so the best plan is to hard boil your eggs first (p. 36) and then get out your paint box and paint designs on the cooked eggs with a brush. There are some suggestions on page 79 for you, or, better still, make up some designs of your own.

Is there a birthday coming along in your family soon? If so, why don't you make the birthday cake. Double the recipe in Chapter IX, and, instead of cooking the batter in little patty pans, make it in three sandwich tins for a layer cake. When the cake is done, turn it out and spread filling between the layers and and icing over the top.

CHOCOLATE FILLING

Ingredients	Utensils
4 tablespoons margarine.	A mixing basin.
6 level tablespoons icing sugar.	The sieve.
2 level tablespoons cocoa.	Tablespoon.
A few drops of milk.	Knife.

1. Put the margarine in the basin and stir it until it is soft and creamy.
2. Sift the sugar and cocoa together and add to the margarine gradually.
3. Add milk (only a very little) if it seems too stiff to spread.
4. Spread between the layers with the blade of the knife.

WHITE ICING.

Ingredients	Utensils
4 oz. icing sugar.	The sieve.
1 tablespoon milk (about).	A mixing basin.
Few drops vanilla essence.	A tablespoon.
	A knife for spreading.

1. Sift the icing sugar into the basin.

2. Add the milk a little at a time until your icing is the right consistency for spreading. (If you add too much milk by mistake, you can always sift in a little more icing sugar.)
3. Add the vanilla.
4. Spread over the top of your cake with the blade of the knife.

You probably have your own ideas about arranging candles on the top. If it's a summer birthday, a good idea is to make a wreath of flowers round the base of the cake, which covers up any untidy crummy bits.

The last day of October is called All Hallows E'en, and that is the night when witches and ghosts are apt to be about. A Hallowe'en party is fun. Set a lighted Jack o'lantern in the window for your guests to see as they come up the path, or have it in the hall to welcome them as they come in the front door. Here's how you make it:

Buy a good round pumpkin and cut out from the top a section about 6 inches across (keep this all in one piece like a lid, with the stem end for a handle). Scoop out the seeds and the pulp with a big spoon. Draw a fine face on the side of your pumpkin and with a sharp knife cut out the eyes and nose and mouth. Leave one or two teeth to make a good grin. Set a short candle inside, fixing it in firmly, light it, put on the lid, and there you are.

A nice sweet to serve at your party would be pumpkin pie. You could make it with meat from a pumpkin or an ordinary marrow:

PUMPKIN PIE

Ingredients	Utensils
½ pint prepared pumpkin or marrow.	A sharp knife.
2 oz. sugar, brown if possible.	A teaspoon.
1 level teaspoon cinnamon.	A tablespoon.
¼ teaspoon ginger.	A pint jug.
¼ teaspoon salt.	Scales.
2 eggs, fresh or dried, re-constituted.	The sieve.
	A wooden mixing spoon.
	Mixing basin.
¼ pint of scalded milk.	Flan tin.
½ oz. margarine.	
1 tablespoon treacle.	

1. To prepare the marrow or pumpkin, steam or bake 2-3 lb. until it is soft—baking is better, as the marrow or pumpkin comes out drier.

2. Strain or mash well, and of course take out the seeds. Measure out ½ pint.

3. Add the sugar, spices, salt and eggs.

4. Melt the margarine in the milk and add to the mixture.

5. Line a flan tin with your best pastry, pour in the marrow mixture and bake. The oven should be quite hot for the first 10 minutes to cook the crust; then reduce the heat and cook for 30-40 minutes in a slow oven.

6. This is a custard mixture and must not boil in the oven; it must not even simmer. Test it with the blade of a knife; when the knife comes out clean the pie is done.

Do you help mix the Christmas pudding in your house? It is great fun to give the stiff dough a stir and make a wish. Near Christmas itself you might make some mince pies.

MINCEMEAT

Ingredients	Utensils
1 lb. apples after peeling and coring.	A sharp small knife.
1 lb. dried fruit (including raisins, sultanas, dates and currants).	A teaspoon.
	A tablespoon.
	The scales.
4 oz. sugar.	A big mixing basin.
3 oz. suet or margarine.	The mincer *or* the chopping bowl and chopper.
2 level teaspoons mixed spice.	Empty jam jars.
$\frac{1}{2}$ teaspoon salt.	Greaseproof paper and string.
$\frac{1}{2}$ teaspoon lemon essence.	
$\frac{1}{2}$ teaspoon almond essence.	
6 tablespoons vinegar.	
1 level tablespoon marmalade.	

1. Clean the fruit, take the stones out of the raisins and dates and chop them up small or mince them.

2. Peel and core the apples, then grate them or put them through the mincer.

3. Mix all these ingredients together in a basin, adding sugar, salt, spice, and marmalade.

4. If suet is used, let it be shredded, grated or chopped finely before adding; if margarine, melt it and pour over the mixture, then stir it in.

5. Add the essences to the vinegar, add to the other ingredients and give one more stir.
6. Put into small jars; tie covers of greaseproof paper over the tops.

This quantity makes a good 2½ lb. of mincemeat and it should keep a couple of months.

If oranges are about, you will be able to improve the flavour of the mincemeat by adding half a rind grated and perhaps a teaspoonful of juice instead of the marmalade.

Use your pastry recipe (p. 58) and roll it out in the usual way. Then cut into circles about 3 inches across. Put a heaping table-spoonful of mincemeat in the middle. Moisten the edges of the pastry circle with a little cold water and then fold over to make a half-circle and pinch the two edges together. You can decorate the edges by pressing down with the prongs of a fork. This looks pretty and helps prevent the mincemeat running out.

Prick the top with a fork in several places and bake in a hot oven for 20 minutes or until the pastry is a delicate brown.

CHAPTER XXI

Cook-books and Recipes

NOW, having gone through this book and made the dishes in it, you should be able to use the recipes in any cook-book you like. In fact, I suggest that you start a collection of cook-books. The first I advise is not so much a book of recipes as a book which will help you to understand the principles of cooking and which will make it easy for you to follow quite complicated recipes. This is The A.B.C. of Cookery (1s.; published by the Ministry of Food).

Then from there I should go on to rather more general books. There are very good ones published by the various companies that make cooking stoves. The Radiation Cooking Book (3s.; obtainable from Radiation, Ltd., 7 Stratford Place, W.1) is an excellent one; so is The Aga Cook-book (2s. 6d.; Aga Heat, Ltd., 20 North Audley Street, W.1).

After that you will want to find more out-of-the-way recipes; such cook-books you will have to look round for, choosing just what appeals to you. Recipes from different parts of Britain (shortbread from Scotland, hotpot from Lancashire, and so forth) are great fun to collect, and recipes from foreign countries are always fascinating.

Best of all, make a cook-book of your own. Get a loose-leaf notebook and divide it into sections; soups, meat, cakes, puddings and so forth, and copy in any recipe you particularly like. If you have something specially good to eat at a friend's house, ask your hostess how the dish was made, write it down and copy it into your book when you get home. Cut out recipes from magazines and newspapers. Try them first and then, if you like them, paste them into your book.

85

And here, to finish with, are a few more recipes of my own. Some of them are American (Hamburgers, Johnny cake, and so forth) and, with the French Vegetable Soup in Chapter X, you see you already have started your foreign collection.

BREAKFAST DISHES

PORRIDGE

1 pint of water *or*
½ pint milk and ½ pint water.
4 oz. quick-cooking oats.
¼ tablespoon salt.

Put the water or milk and water into a saucepan and add the salt. Don't let it boil over while your back is turned. Bring to the boil, and while it is boiling add the oats very gradually, stirring all the time and keeping the water boiling.

Reduce the heat and cook until the porridge is nice and thick —about 5 minutes. Keep stirring, so that it won't burn. If you like, you can make it in the top of a double saucepan —then, once the oats have been added to the boiling liquid and stirred well, you can finish the porridge by leaving it for 15 minutes over the boiling water in the bottom half of the saucepan.

SCRAMBLED EGGS

1 dessertspoon margarine.
4 eggs.
½ teaspoon salt.
⅛ teaspoon pepper.
4 tablespoons milk.

Melt the margarine in the top of a double saucepan over boiling water. Mix the eggs well in a basin and add the salt and pepper. Stir in the milk. Pour the mixture into

86

the saucepan. With a wooden spoon, as the egg cooks and thickens, keep stirring it and scraping it down from the sides to the middle. This method of scrambling eggs over hot water is much easier than directly over the flame. Eggs should always have slow, gentle cooking, and this way you don't run the danger of dry, tough scrambled eggs. Takes 10 minutes' cooking time.

This recipe makes four rather small portions. You can stretch the amount by adding two slices of bread cut into small pieces and lightly fried in dripping or bacon fat.

You can do many interesting things to scrambled eggs. Try adding 1 tablespoon chopped parsley, *or* 1 tablespoon chopped chives, *or* ¼ lb. mushrooms chopped and fried first.

LUNCH OR SUPPER DISHES

CHEESE MACARONI

4 oz. macaroni.
3 pints water.
2 teaspoons salt.
3 oz. cheese, grated or cut up very small.
1 dessertspoonful margarine or dripping.
½ pint cup of white sauce (p. 62).
2 oz. breadcrumbs.

Put the water in a large saucepan, add the salt, and bring to the boil. Break the macaroni into short lengths (about 1 inch), and drop into the water gradually so that boiling doesn't stop. Boil for 20 minutes or until the macaroni is soft, stirring occasionally with a fork so that the macaroni doesn't stick.

When the macaroni is done, strain in a large colander. Then pour over and through the macaroni 3 cups of cold water; this will prevent the macaroni from being sticky. Now mix

87

the cooked macaroni, the white sauce and the cheese together and put in a casserole. Melt the margarine, add the breadcrumbs and mix together lightly. Sprinkle the crumbs over the top of the macaroni right to the edges of the casserole. Put in a medium oven for 10 minutes or until the crumbs are golden brown.

BLUSHING BUNNY

2 level tablespoons plain flour.
1 level tablespoon margarine.
2 level tablespoons grated cheese.
4 tomatoes.
4 oz. breakfastcup milk (8 tablespoons).
½ teaspoon sugar.
½ teaspoon salt.
A few grains pepper.
⅛ teaspoon bicarbonate of soda.
4 large slices toast.

Peel and slice the tomatoes, place in a saucepan and simmer 10 minutes in their own juice with the salt, pepper and sugar. Make a white sauce of the margarine, flour and milk and stir in the grated cheese. Add the soda to the tomatoes. Combine the two mixtures and pour over the toast. Serve at once.

This is also very good made in the winter with bottled tomatoes.

SPECIAL HAMBURGERS

1 lb. minced beef or stewing steak.
3 oz. soft breadcrumbs.
4 oz. cup milk (about 8 tablespoons).
1 tablespoon tomato ketchup.
1 teaspoon Worcester sauce.
1 teaspoon salt.
Dash of pepper.
1 medium onion, chopped fine.

Combine breadcrumbs, milk, ketchup and Worcester sauce.
Let this stand for 5 minutes. If you use stewing steak, put
it through the mincer, and the onion with it. If meat is
already minced, chop the onion as fine as you can. Add
meat, onion, salt and pepper to the breadcrumb mixture
and mix very well. Form into flat cakes about $\frac{1}{2}$ inch thick.
Fry in bacon fat (very little is needed; only a teaspoon to
grease the pan before the fat in the meat begins to melt).
Have the pan hot to begin with and then cook slowly for
about 8-10 minutes on first side, turn and cook 5-7
minutes on the other. Don't overcook, as the meat will
get dry and tough.

Some people make a gravy with the fat left in the pan and
serve with the hamburgers.

STUFFED MARROW

A medium-size marrow.
2 slices of bread.
2 onions.
1 dessertspoon chopped parsley.
4 oz. cup stock or milk (8 tablespoons).
$\frac{1}{2}$ teaspoon salt.
A few grains pepper.
1 tablespoon grated cheese *or*
2 tablespoons minced cooked meat.
2 oz. dripping.

Tear the bread into small crumbs and put it in a basin and
soak with the stock or milk.

Peel the marrow and cut it in half lengthwise. Take out all
the seeds and stringy bits.

Chop the onion finely and add it to the soaked crumbs. Add
the salt, pepper and parsley, and the grated cheese or the
minced meat and mix well.

Put the stuffing in one half of the marrow and lay the other
half on top like a lid. Tie a piece of string round the two

halves to keep them from slipping apart. Melt the dripping in the roasting pan and lay the marrow in. Bake in a hot oven, basting with dripping every 10 minutes. Cook for 30 minutes or until the marrow is soft when pricked with a fork.

To serve, lift the marrow on to a hot platter, cut the string and remove it, and decorate the dish with a few sprigs of parsley.

VEGETABLES

BOILED POTATOES

Allow 2 medium-size potatoes for each person or 2 lb. of new potatoes for four people.

Scrub the potatoes well and put them into boiling salted water, with 2 teaspoons of salt for each quart of water. The water should just cover the potatoes.

Cook with the lid on for from 20 to 30 minutes (depending on the size of your potatoes). Keep the water boiling fast, but test the potatoes with a fork as soon as you think they may be getting done. Don't let them overcook and get mushy. When they are soft, pour away the water. Put the pan with the potatoes back over the heat (*very low heat*). Shake the pan back and forth for a minute to dry them off. Then take from the stove and either serve them in their skins or peel them and serve with a little chopped parsley sprinkled over them. To peel hot potatoes, spear them on your fork, hold them upright and then peel off the skin with a small, sharp knife.

MASHED POTATOES

Boil and peel 5 or 6 old potatoes (not new ones) and put them back in the warm saucepan. Use a large fork or a potato-masher and beat until they are white and fluffy. In a small saucepan heat 2 or 3 tablespoons milk and 1 dessertspoon margarine. Add the hot milk and melted margarine to the potatoes and beat again. The great secret of mashing potatoes is to have the milk hot and the potatoes as hot as can be managed. Also be sure the potatoes are thoroughly cooked, otherwise you get hard little lumps in the mashed potatoes.

Add salt and pepper to taste and pile lightly in your warmed serving dish. Take the back of a fork and make light lines over the top; and a dash of paprika looks pretty.

GLAZED CARROTS

4 large carrots *or*
1 bunch of small carrots.
$\frac{1}{2}$ teaspoon salt.
$\frac{1}{2}$ teaspoon sugar.
1 teaspoon margarine.

Wash the carrots, scrubbing them well with a vegetable brush. If they are very old and grubby, scrape the outsides with a sharp knife.

Cut the old carrots in small pieces, leave the young ones whole. In a saucepan put 1 inch of water, bring it to the boil, add the salt and sugar and the chopped carrots or the whole young ones. Add the margarine, bring to the boil again and then turn the flame down so the carrots just boil steadily. Put the lid on, but look at them frequently to make sure the water hasn't boiled away, and stir them to keep them from catching on the bottom. You may have to add a little more water. Test with a fork to try if they are done. They will take 15 or 20 minutes to cook. And, by then, the water should have been nearly boiled away and all the goodness is still left in the carrots.

If you have got a little water left in the pan, take the lid off, turn the flame up and stir the carrots until the water is boiled away.

Serve in a warm dish; and a little parsley chopped over the top is very pretty.

29/9/57.

CABBAGE

1 cabbage weighing about 2 lb.
1 teaspoon salt.
Water.

Take off the very coarse or bruised outside leaves of the cabbage. Cut off the tough part of the stem.

Cut the cabbage in half from top to bottom and cut out the tough stem inside, but only the stem. Wash it thoroughly in plenty of cold water.

Now lay it on a chopping board and cut it across into shreds about 1 inch wide.

In a large saucepan put about 1 inch of water and the salt and bring it to the boil. When it is boiling put in the chopped cabbage. Put the lid on the saucepan and cook for 10 minutes, stirring occasionally. This way, the cabbage stays crisp and bright green instead of going limp and tasteless.

PEAS

1 lb. peas in the pod.
$\frac{1}{4}$ teaspoon salt.
$\frac{1}{2}$ teaspoon sugar.
A sprig of mint if you have it.
Water.

Remove the peas from their pods. (Press down on the blunt end with your thumb and they will split open.)

Put a little water in a saucepan, add the sugar and salt and, when the water is boiling, the peas.

Cook gently for 5 minutes, or until the peas are soft. You test them by taking one up in a spoon or on a fork and eating it. If they are cooked too long, they get tough again. Old peas may take longer, though—up to 20 minutes. The water should be all boiled away when the peas are done.

TOMATOES

1 lb. tomatoes (either green or ripe).
2 teaspoons dripping.
Salt and pepper.

Rub half the dripping over the bottom of a shallow cake tin or casserole. Cut the tomatoes in half and set them in the tin cut side up. Put a tiny bit of dripping on each one and sprinkle lightly with salt and pepper. Set in a hot oven or under the toasting grill. They will take 10 minutes to cook in the oven, or 5 minutes under the grill. But watch them to see they don't burn.

ONIONS IN WHITE SAUCE

6 large onions.
1 pint of white sauce.
1 teaspoon salt.
Water.

Cut the root end off the onions and take off the outside skin (just the thin, brown, papery one).

Put enough water to cover the onions in a saucepan, add the salt and bring to the boil. Put in the onions. The time onions will take to cook depends on their size. Small ones take about 20 minutes; big ones will take twice as long. You test them with a fork to see if they are done.

While they are cooking, make your white sauce and make it rather thick (using less milk than the recipe on p. 62: then, when the onions are done, you can thin it down by adding a little of the water in which the onions were cooked, which will give your sauce a lovely flavour.)

93

Put the onions in a warm casserole. Pour the sauce over and serve.

This is a nice dish, because it can be made way ahead of time, and then heated up in a casserole in the oven for lunch or supper.

6/10/57.

SOUPS

ONION SOUP

4 onions.
3 level tablespoons dripping or bacon fat.
1 pint stock *or*
1 pint water and 1 teaspoon meat or vegetable extract.
2 tablespoons grated cheese.
4 slices toast.

Slice the onions thinly and fry them very slowly in the dripping. They should be cooked until they are soft and yellow. They should not get brown. Add the stock or water and extract and simmer for 30 minutes.

Make the toast and grate the cheese.

To serve, put a slice of toast in each individual soup dish and pour the soup over. Sprinkle the grated cheese on top iust before serving.

POTATO SOUP

2/8/58.

1½ oz. bacon—that is, 1 rasher.
1 onion or 1 leek.
1½ lb. potatoes—that is, 4 medium potatoes.
¾ pint boiling water.
½ pint of milk.
1 level teaspoon salt.
Few grains pepper.
1 level tablespoon chopped parsley.

Peel and cut up the potatoes (about the size of sugar lumps), chop onion finely, cut the bacon up small. Fry the bacon in the saucepan in which the soup is going to be made.

94

When it is crisp, add the onion and potatoes. Add the water, bring to the boil, cover and allow to simmer 10-15 minutes till the potatoes are tender. Add the milk and cook for 5 minutes longer. Season with salt and pepper and sprinkle with the chopped parsley.

This is quickly made, and as you see, doesn't call for any exotic ingredients, but all the same it's a delicious soup.

✓ 18·8·63.

PUDDINGS

SOFT CUSTARD

1 pint milk.
3 eggs.
2 tablespoons sugar.
¼ teaspoon salt.
½ teaspoon vanilla extract.

Heat the milk in the top of a double saucepan. Break the eggs into a basin or your pint jug and beat them slightly. Add the sugar and salt and mix well. Pour on gradually the hot milk and stir thoroughly. Return the mixture to the top of the double saucepan and cook over hot water, *Do not boil!* stirring all the time with a wooden spoon. Cook for about 7 minutes. Add the vanilla. The custard is done when the mixture just coats the back of the spoon.

BAKED CUSTARD

2/8/58.

1 pint milk.
3–4 eggs.
2 tablespoons sugar.
¼ teaspoon salt.
½ teaspoon vanilla extract or lemon or almond essence.

Heat the milk and add to the beaten eggs sugar and salt, as in boiled soft custard. Add the flavouring and pour the mixture into a greased casserole or pudding dish. Stand this in a pan of hot water in the oven. The water should come halfway up the sides of the custard dish and should not get hot enough to boil. Bake in a moderate oven until set, 30 to 45 minutes. The custard is done when a knife inserted into it comes out clean.

APPLE SAUCE

8 large apples.
1 cup water.
¼ teaspoon salt.
2–4 tablespoons sugar.
¼ teaspoon grated nutmeg.

Wash the apples, cut them into quarters and remove the core. Do not peel. Put in a saucepan with the water and salt. Cook slowly until they are soft. Rub through a coarse sieve and add the sugar and spice. The amount of sugar and nutmeg varies according to the apples. You will have to use your own judgment about how much to add.

MILK PUDDING

1½ pints milk. _less milk_
2 tablespoons rice. _more rice_ } needed.
½ teaspoon salt.
5 oz. sugar.
A little grated lemon rind.
1 teaspoon margarine.

Light the oven and set it slow. Grease the casserole with the margarine. Put the rice into the sieve and let cold water from the tap run through it for a minute. Put the rice and the sugar and the salt into the casserole. Pour in the milk. Add the grated lemon rind and stir it all together, and put in the oven. Stir three times during the first hour of baking, and then leave it alone to form the nice brown skin on the top. But be sure the oven stays *slow*; the milk mustn't boil, ever.

96

BEST BREAD PUDDING

3 slices of stale bread, cut thick.
2 level tablespoons of margarine.
1 egg, fresh or reconstituted.
2 tablespoons of marmalade or jam.
1 level dessertspoon of sugar.
¼ teaspoon of cinnamon.
1 pint of milk (household or fresh).

Cut your slices of bread up into shapes to fit a medium deep casserole, so that you will have two or three layers. Spread the pieces of bread with the margarine and the marmalade and lay them in the dish, spread side down, in layers. (You might keep back just a small bit of the margarine; do not spread it all on, but be generous with the marmalade.) Now mix the reconstituted egg with the milk and stir well. Pour over the bread in the dish. And do not worry if it looks awfully runny. Mix the sugar with the cinnamon and sprinkle it over the top of the pudding, and if you saved any of the margarine, dot it over the top too. Now let the pudding stand a few minutes so that the bread may soak up the milk. (This will take care of that runny look.) Then bake in a very slow oven—really slow because, of course, this is a custard mixture, and it is fatal to let the oven get so hot that the pudding boils or even simmers—for ¼ hour with a lid on it. Take the lid off and finish baking for another ½ hour, and you will have a delicious crusty top on a nice firm pudding.

COOKIES AND CAKES

AMERICAN COOKIES

2 oz. margarine.
4 oz. sugar.
1 egg, fresh or reconstituted.
1 dessertspoon milk.
¼ teaspoon vanilla.

¼ teaspoon salt.
6 oz. plain flour.
1 level teaspoon baking powder.
½ teaspoon cinnamon.
½ teaspoon nutmeg.
} dry ingredients

Cream the margarine and the sugar. Stir in the egg. Sift the dry ingredients together and add to the first mixture alternatively with the milk. Add the vanilla. Roll out $\frac{1}{4}$ inch thick on a floured board. Cut into rounds with a scone-cutter or with a wineglass dipped in flour. Bake on a greased baking sheet in a moderately hot oven 8 minutes.

Makes two dozen cookies.

JOHNNY CAKE

5 oz. of semolina.
1 teacup of plain flour.
3 level teaspoons baking powder.
1 level tablespoon of dried egg, dry. ⎫ dry
1 level dessertspoon sugar. ⎬ ingredients
$\frac{3}{4}$ teaspoon of salt. ⎭
8 oz. of milk.
2 tablespoons of cold water.
2 tablespoons of melted margarine.

Mix and sift the dry ingredients; add the milk and melted margarine and cold water. Bake either in little cake tins or in a shallow greased cake tin 20 minutes in quite a hot oven: the top of your johnny cake should be golden brown when it's done. Eat for tea with butter and jam.

Note. This is a wartime version. Proper johnny cake uses American corn-meal in place of the semolina.

9/10/57.

SPONGE CAKE

4 eggs.
8 oz. castor sugar.
2 tablespoons cold water.
1 level tablespoon lemon juice or vinegar.
1 level teaspoon vanilla.
4 oz. flour.
$1\frac{1}{4}$ teaspoon baking powder.
$\frac{1}{4}$ teaspoon salt.

Separate the egg yolk and whites. Beat the white until stiff and add 4 tablespoons of the sugar. Whisk the yolks with the water and lemon juice or vinegar, until the mixture is very thick. Add the vanilla and the rest of the sugar. Add the whites to the yolk mixture and mix them together by cutting the mixture with a knife, not a spoon.

Sift the dry ingredients and cut and fold into the eggs. Do not beat or stir.

Pour into sandwich tins or a cake tin with straight sides and bake in a moderate oven for 30 minutes or until the cake is done.

GINGERBREAD

12 oz. black treacle.
$2\frac{1}{2}$ oz. margarine, lard or chicken fat.
5 oz. boiling water.
10 oz. flour.
$\frac{1}{2}$ teaspoon salt.
$1\frac{1}{2}$ level teaspoons bicarbonate of soda.
1 level teaspoon cinnamon.
$\frac{1}{2}$ teaspoon ground cloves.
$\frac{1}{4}$ teaspoon grated nutmeg.

Put the treacle and fat in a saucepan and bring to the boil. Sift the dry ingredients together. Add the boiling water to the treacle and fat, and add the dry ingredients. (All in the saucepan; this makes very little washing up.) Mix thoroughly, beating well. Pour into a shallow greased cake pan and bake for 30 to 40 minutes in a moderate oven.

Index of Recipes

AMERICAN COOKIES, 97
Apple sauce, 96
Apples, baked, 22

BACON AND EGGS, FRIED, 76
Baked apples, 22
   custard, 95
   potatoes, 25
Blackberry jam, 70
Blushing bunny, 88
Boiled eggs, 23
   potatoes, 90
Bread pudding, best, 97

CABBAGE, 92
Cake, 41
   Johnny, 98
   sponge, 98
Carrots, glazed, 91
Cauliflower cheese, 62
Cheese, cauliflower, 62
   macaroni, 87
Chocolate filling, 80
   fudge, 67
Cocoa, 30
Coffee, 29
Cookies, American, 97
Croutons, 47
Custard, baked, 95
   soft, 95

DRESSING, FRENCH, 38

EGGS AND BACON, FRIED, 76
   scrambled, 86
   stuffed, 73

FILLING, CHOCOLATE, 80
French dressing, 38
   vegetable soup, 46
Fried eggs and bacon, 76
Fudge, 67

GINGERBREAD, 99
Glazed carrots, 91

HAMBURGERS, SPECIAL, 88
Hot buttered toast, 15

ICING, WHITE, 80

JAM, BLACKBERRY, 70
   tarts, 58
Jelly, squash, 55
Johnny cake, 98

LEMONADE, 31

MACARONI CHEESE, 87
Marrow, stuffed, 89
Mashed potatoes, 90
Milk pudding, 96
Mincemeat, 83

ONION SOUP, 94
Onions in white sauce, 93
Oven stew, 50

PANCAKES, 78
Peas, 92
Porridge, 86
Potatoes, baked, 25
   boiled, 90
   mashed, 90
Potato soup, 94
Pudding, best bread, 97
   milk, 96
   semolina, 51
Pumpkin pie, 82

SALAD, SUMMER, 36
   winter, 37

Salmon in white sauce with buttered
    crumbs, 65
Sandwiches, 43
Sauce, apple, 96
   white, 62
Sausages, 54
Scones, 18
Scrambled eggs, 86
Semolina pudding, 51
Soft custard, 95
Soup, French vegetable, 46
   onion, 94
   potato, 94
Special hamburgers, 88
Sponge cake, 98
Squash jelly, 55

Stew, oven, 50
Stuffed eggs, 73
   marrow, 89

Tarts, jam, 58
Tea, 14
Toast, hot buttered, 15
Tomatoes, 93

Vegetable soup, French, 46

White icing, 80
   sauce, 62

Mushroom + liver Sausage spread.

gredients: 4 oz chopped mushrooms.
            ½ oz butter
            8 oz liver sausage
            ½ Teaspoon Worcester sauce
            salt if required : mayonnaise to bind.

op washed mushrooms finely + lightly fry in butter until tender ~ abt minutes. mix prepared mushrooms with liver sausage + seasonings enough mayonnaise to bind. Use as a spread for sandwiches. Also elicious when put in tiny heaps on potato crisps.

Mushroom vol-au-vent.

gred: 8 oz mushrooms
         small vol-au-vent cases.

         ½ pint white sauce
         milk to cook the mushrooms
         salt
         a little lemon juice.

For the sauce: 2 oz butter
              2 oz flour
              ½ pint milk in which mushrooms were cooked
              1 yolk of egg
              2 tablespoonsful of cream
              salt + pepper.
              a little nutmeg.

wipe mushrooms. put into a pan with enough milk to cover add salt + lemon juice, cook till tender. abt 8 - 10 minutes cook with lid on. Strain mushrooms + keep milk. melt butter in a saucepan, add flour, mix till smooth but do not let it brown, add gradually, stirring till well blended. Add mushrooms finely sliced, bring to boil, simmer a few minutes to cook the flour. Remove from heat + stir in the beaten egg yolk, cream, salt, pepper, + nutmeg. Warm the vol-au-vent cases + fill with the mixture. dust the tops with cayenne.

Mushroom Tartlets.

Make a quantity of crisp short pastry shells. Into each fit a cooked mushroom of suitable size. Fill with scrambled eggs mixed with chopped ham. Sprinkle with chopped parsley.

Write for further recipes to:

Mushroom Growers' Association,

    Agriculture House,

        Knightsbridge

           S.W.1.